# Measuring Performance

## Using the new metrics

## to deploy strategy

## and improve performance

by Dr. Bob Frost

REVISED EDITION
Copyright © 2000
by Bob Frost


All rights reserved. No portion of this publication may be reproduced in any form or by any means, electronic or mechanical, without written permission from the copyright owner.

# Contents

# Introduction

Perhaps you're a manager or executive who wants to improve performance, is short on time, and needs a practical handle on performance metrics.

Maybe you also want out of the data jungle—that familiar place with too many data points and not enough real information. Perhaps you want gauges to measure important trends and levers you can pull to move things along or change direction. In short, tools you can use to align efforts and improve results.

That's what this book is about.

It's about metrics, to be sure. But it's also about leadership and how metrics figure in the job of implementing strategy and improving performance.

In these few pages, you'll find a straightforward overview of performance metrics, a model for strategy-based performance management, and insights distilled from many years in practice—all summarized as simply and briefly as possible. In later chapters, we will address some of the challenges and controversies you'll encounter in performance metrics.

– Bob Frost

# Part 1

---

# The New Metrics

- A New Discipline

- A Balanced Scorecard

- Metrics & Leadership

- Assess Your Metrics

# A New Discipline

Let's start at the beginning. Management is about getting things done. And in purposeful organizations, it's increasingly understood that "what gets measured, gets done." So it's really no surprise that leaders today are very concerned about exactly what is measured.

You could truthfully say that measurement is becoming a new discipline for managers—a new part of the job. For some, it will require new skills and know-how. For example, you've probably seen sophisticated financial measures like Economic Value Added (EVA), as well as multidimensional performance metrics coming from Balanced Scorecards, Enterprise Resource Planning (ERP), customer measures, Activity Based Costing (ABC), Process Management and other approaches.

Only a few short years ago, everyone simply tracked financial results and nothing more. What happened to change that? Customer demands and competition escalated, and time became compressed. Everything had to be better, faster, cheaper. Under this pressure, it became clear to managers that financial systems helped them manage budgets, but not the business itself. Financial metrics were not detailed or targeted enough to help them steer business activities in real time, day to day. On top of all this, financial measures were invariably "lagging" rather than "leading" indicators. They were after the fact—more like a rearview mirror than a windshield or steering wheel.

About the same time, the quality movement, reengineering, and process management all demonstrated other kinds of metrics that, used systematically, could drive change, strengthen the business, and even help leaders create better financial returns. Performance management came to mean objective, measure-based performance management.

Then strategy made a comeback. Leaders realized that charting a course and applying a strategy to beat competitors still counted, even in chaotic business environments. To drive change and implement strategies quickly, leading organizations began tying their performance metrics to their strategic plans. Performance management came to mean measure-based, strategy-driven performance management.

During this period, large data warehousing projects (such as Enterprise Resource Planning) were also underway, managing the sourcing and distribution of business information to make it available anytime, anywhere. These efforts uncovered needs for new types of information as well as better metrics to track

*"The new measures are predictive and prescriptive."*
–J. M. Sieger

7.

performance; designing these metrics and reports became one of the critical pinch points in completing ERP projects successfully.

What's the bottom line? Just that performance metrics—solid, well-founded ones—are no longer optional. They are rapidly becoming a new discipline for leaders at all levels. Those who master performance metrics gain significant leverage in aligning efforts, implementing strategies, and driving results.

## The Metrics Revolution

| THE OLD METRICS | THE NEW METRICS |
|---|---|
| Primarily financial | Multidimensional |
| After the fact | Mid-course steering |
| Control and report | Align effort, create value |
| Not actionable | Line of sight to action |
| Earnings & taxes | Implement strategy |
| Within functional areas | Manage across functions |
| Manage input costs | Manage output value |

8.

Measuring Performance

9.

# The Balanced Scorecard

What do the new measures of performance look like? While traditional business metrics focused on a single perspective, financial, the new metrics are multidimensional—looking at several different aspects of business at the same time. In other words, they reflect the reality and complexity of business situations. After all, unless you measure all sides of a problem, how do you know whether the dent you make in a problem actually shrinks it or just creates a new bulge somewhere else? So the new metrics are multidimensional rather than unidimensional. They try to cover all the factors that really matter in implementing strategy and improving performance.

The Balanced Scorecard is a good example of what the new metrics look like. In fact, much of the credit for the new thinking in performance metrics goes to Drs. Robert Kaplan and David Norton, developers of the Balanced Scorecard concept. Kaplan and Norton studied the trends in performance metrics at leading organizations and published one of the first models to organize the new breed of metrics into a coherent structure—the Balanced Scorecard.

The Balanced Scorecard groups metrics into four categories: Financial, Customer, Internal Processes, and Learning & Growth. Each of the four categories contains specific performance measures aimed at answering key questions about one important dimension of business.

## Balanced Scorecard Model

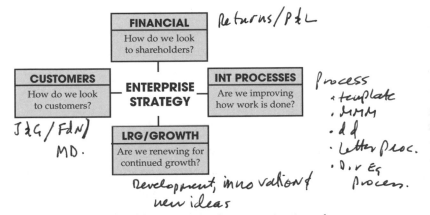

*[handwritten annotations: Returns/P&L; Process, template, MMM, dd, Letter Proc., Dir Eq Process; JdG/FdN/ MD.; Development, innovation/ new ideas]*

A Balanced Scorecard for a particular organization, for example, might include several Financial measures, such as *Return on Net Assets*, *Total Shareholder Return*, and others. The Customers category might include *Service Satisfaction*, *Wait Time*, *On-Time Delivery*, etc. The Internal Processes category would offer such indicators as *Product Assembly Cost* and *Productivity*. *Agility* and *Rate of Patent Approvals* might be performance indicators in the Learning/Growth category.

The Financial category deals primarily with the past and what you have achieved for shareholders. Metrics in the Learning/Growth category are forward-looking. Customer measures look outside your enterprise and Process measures focus internally on efficient work processes. A traditional Balanced Scorecard, then, organizes metrics so the historical view is balanced by metrics about the future, and the external view is balanced by metrics about internal performance. All give you valuable information about the health of your organization, and no single perspective is enough by itself. That's the "balance" in the Balanced Scorecard.

Although the Balanced Scorecard is a popular and widely used starting point, one should apply it cautiously. It's not a one-size garment but, rather, a model that will probably require alterations to fit your situation properly. In actual practice, you'll find far more "modified" Balanced Scorecards than pure applications of the original design.

# Metrics and Leadership

The leader's job today involves processing information and taking action. Lots of information and lots of action. This applies at every level in a modern organization, and it applies whether the leadership role is filled by a single individual or by team processes.

In part, it's like running a big machine where you monitor gauges, make decisions, and pull levers that produce better output. With gauges to read and levers to pull, you make the machine perform.

But another aspect of the leadership role, the part about creating change, can be quite different. It's more like carrying Jello without a bowl; there aren't any handles. Getting good performance metrics is like attaching handles so you can grab onto something and move the Jello in the right direction.

Performance metrics go a long way toward providing the gauges, levers, and handles to move your organization in the right direction. In fact, they play crucial roles in four of your most significant activities as a leader:

1. **Reporting performance.** You calibrate and summarize information about your areas of responsibility, and receive such reports from others. Such reports include resources consumed and the value created. Rich, comprehensive performance

14.

## "FACT - BASED MANAGEMENT"

metrics such as *Order-to-Delivery Cycle Time, Patents Per Year, Customer Satisfaction, Productivity* and others show the value created and ensure that your people get full credit for what they've accomplished.

2.  **Making decisions.** Information reduces uncertainty, tells where action should be taken, and inspires confidence. It enables you to practice fact-based management. For example, process measures such as cycle times and inventory at each stage of production can tell you where there's a performance bottleneck, as well as the payback you'd get from alleviating it.

> *"An executive is by profession a decision maker. Uncertainty is the opponent. Overcoming it is the objective."*
> –J. McDonald

3.  **Implementing strategy.** Whether you are responsible for an entire line of business or a small department, as a leader you're essential in translating the strategy of your organization into tangible action and tangible value. Properly developed, your performance metrics will be directly based on your organization's strategic direction—they will represent the broad goals of your enterprise in concrete ways that properly align and direct activities. There is no more essential and valuable step in performance management than translating the overall direction of your organization into concrete and meaningful terms that people understand.

15.

4. **Improving performance.** Short term, one of the most important components of the leader's job is improving performance—day to day, it's much of what a leader's job is really about. To do it, you align effort behind the right tasks, rationalize resources, manage accountabilities, and improve work processes. In each of these leadership activities, valid performance metrics give the information and leverage to get the job done. Here again, metrics enable you to manage by fact; without them, you're left to lead with charm and personality.

*Yep .*

## Metrics and Leadership

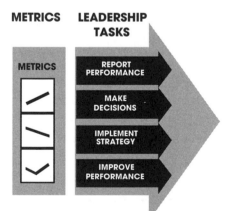

What can you personally gain by deploying balanced performance metrics in your area of responsibility? For starters, you can achieve fact-based decision making, clearer reporting, well-executed strategy, and improved performance. As a bonus, sharing performance metrics widely throughout an organization helps everyone learn exactly how to help the organization succeed. When a concept like "empowering your employees" fails, it's generally because the encouragement to take new actions is not coupled with clear feedback and performance metrics that tell what are good actions and what aren't.

Designing and implementing good performance metrics does require time and effort. But, after all, what's it worth to have handles on the Jello?

# Assess Your Metrics

How do you know whether your current performance metrics are the right ones for your business or functional area? You could have them audited by an expert, but you can do much the same yourself. Examine carefully what they're supposed to do and compare it to what they're actually doing for you.

Consider your metrics as a group and rate them as follows:

1 = *No value on this goal*
2 = *Some help on this goal*
3 = *Quite helpful on this goal*
4 = *Extremely valuable on this goal*

How well do your performance metrics:

☑ Translate your business strategy into concrete action?

☑ Align departments behind common goals?

☑ Fully reflect what your stakeholders care about?

☑ Provide the leverage to create change?

☑ Balance leading and lagging indicators?

☑ Balance strategic and operational indicators?

☑ Enhance your ability to compete in the future?

☑ Drive improvements in how work is performed?

☑ Include internal and external benchmarks to judge performance?

18.

Total your ratings. A total less than 18 suggests your metrics are falling down on the job. If your total is 18–27, there's solid value in your metrics but also room for improvement. Totals over 27 suggest your metrics are among the best.

The questions in this evaluation represent the kind of help you have a right to expect from your metrics. Any you didn't mark a 3 or 4 suggest possibilities for improvement.

Should you revise your metrics, tweaking them here or there? Or should you stop patching and rethink the system completely? Your ratings give a summary answer. But you're the one who must ultimately be satisfied with how you track business performance. You and those you report to should have a solid "big picture" understanding of performance in your area.

SOLID "BIG PICTURE" UNDERSTANDING OF PERFORMANCE

20.

# Part 2

---

# What to Measure

- Measurement Models

- Defining Your Metrics

- The Three-Step Method

- Sources of Performance Topics

    - Strategy

    - Stakeholders

    - Snoozing Alligators

# Measurement Models

Some say your measures should be those that help you improve output—make your organization's deliverables better, faster, and cheaper. Few of us would disagree.

How to do it is the issue. Of course, the Balanced Scorecard says you should measure financial results, as well as internal processes, learning/growth, and customer factors.

Some others (Sink and Tuttle, 1989) suggest measuring efficiency, effectiveness, productivity, profitability, quality, innovation, and quality of work life. Others (Thor, 1994) suggest metrics in five categories: profitability, productivity, external quality, internal quality, and other quality.

Still others (Morgantown Energy Technical Center) would have you measure different factors in R & D environments, like objective achievement, cost performance, and technology risk reduction.

The simple truth about these models is this: none of them can tell you exactly what to measure! They have no way of knowing your organization and your industry, let alone your circumstances. At their best, they give you good hints on where to look for performance metrics and how to group your metrics *after* you figure out what they should be. With that thought in mind, let's look into how you define the metrics that are right for your situation.

# Defining Your Metrics

To simplify things, let's divide performance metrics into two types: Primary and Advanced.

**Primary Metrics** address the results you intend to produce and the value you export to others. Financial measures, such as *Total Shareholder Return*, are in this group. So are customer service results, production achievements, and results on specific goals such as cost savings. Primary metrics help you align efforts, manage who's accountable for what, track progress, and report results.

**Advanced Metrics** address the other side of managing performance—the work processes and capabilities of your organization. They help you stop spinning wheels, avoid waste, get more output for your input, and prepare for the future. Examples include measures such as *Product Development Cycle Time, Defect Reduction, Productivity, Organizational Agility*, etc.

Note that, in actual practice, the line between Primary Metrics and Advanced Metrics is a blurred one. The distinction is mainly useful in clarifying concepts. It also reflects a basic fact of life about performance measurement: Virtually all organizations begin by improving their measures of results (Primary Metrics) and only somewhat later take up what we're calling Advanced Metrics.

24.

Next, we'll look into the Three-Step Method used in defining your specific performance indicators.

PRIMARY METRICS

- returns
- P&L

ADVANCED METRICS

? ? ?

- time-wasted study
- ideas?
- ? ? ?

# The Three-Step Method

In actual practice, we've found that defining performance indicators—deciding exactly what to measure—typically involves three distinct steps. In three steps, you can translate a general performance topic into specific performance indicators.

Here's an example. In Step 1, you examine your business strategy to find crucial performance topics (e.g., customer service). In Step 2, you determine where and how you must succeed on each topic, spelling out the where's and how's as a set of Critical Success Factors. For customer service, you might determine that these include quick access, accurate information, and friendly manners. In Step 3, you consider each Critical Success Factor and define specific performance indicators that will track success on it. For your "quick access" factor, these might include *Telephone Wait Time*, *Number of Rings to Answer*, and *Wait Time in Line*.

This method is important in developing proper metrics, so you may want to take a minute to think through a different example on your own. You might try "product development" as a performance topic.

As you see, the three-step process works from the general to the specific—from a performance topic to Critical Success Factors to specific performance indicators. Note that it's important to determine all the Critical Success Factors that apply to a given performance topic.

## Three-Step Method

| STEP 1 → | STEP 2 → | STEP 3 |
|---|---|---|
| Performance Topics | Critical Success Factors | Performance Indicators |
| Financial Performance | | |
| Market Performance | | Phone Wait Time |
| | Quick Access | # Rings to Answer |
| Customer Service | Accurate Info | Wait Time in Store Line |
| | Friendly Tone | |
| Product Development | | |

*✓crucial*

Where do the performance topics come from in the first place? Isn't that the real question? In a way, it is. Much of your success in measuring and improving performance depends on your sources for performance topics. For your Primary Metrics, you'll want to begin with two key sources—your strategy and your stakeholders. These matters are taken up in the next chapters, as well as in a companion volume in this series titled *Crafting Strategy* (ISBN: 0-9702471-0-9).

# Strategy

Almost everyone agrees that your Primary Metrics must reflect your business strategy. It just makes sense that metrics must represent where the enterprise is going—especially since they drive what ultimately gets done. Your strategy and current plan are normally your first sources for performance topics. However, because strategy documents sometimes do not capture all that's important, you'll also want to check your mission and goals as additional sources. When you are defining metrics, the <u>drivers really include your strategy, mission and goals</u>—all the key things you're committed to accomplishing.

Suppose your organization has an ambitious mission to "be the customer's first choice by providing maximum value and timely delivery coupled with customer-oriented service." Or to "be an organization that offers employees the chance to grow as members of high-performing teams." Such goals speak volumes about the areas in which you might measure how you are doing. But they have to be real goals. Be wary of using lofty statements if they are just there for PR purposes.

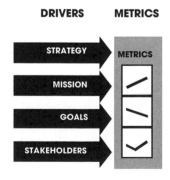

- STRATEGY
- MISSION    "AMBITIOUS MISSION"
- GOALS

Suppose your strategy calls for improving market share by being better, faster, and cheaper. Not as the old joke says, "Better, faster, cheaper … pick any two." But all three—better, faster, and cheaper. Doesn't that give you, right away, some of your most important performance topics, whether you're in Production, Product Development, Marketing, HR, or Legal Services ? Translating these topics from strategy into metrics is not that hard; if it seems totally obscure, you may be too close to the action and could use some assistance from outside your immediate area.

Basing your performance topics on strategy ensures your metrics will be "vertically aligned." That is, they will represent the activities necessary at your level to carry forward the direction of your organization. The company strategy (say, to win more contracts by being a leader in technical competence) will have a specific interpretation in Product Development (such as being

> "A strategy without metrics is just a wish. And metrics that are not aligned with strategy are a waste of time."
> –E. Powell

aggressively up to date on how technology is changing). The point is to focus on where your organization is going and to translate those strategy factors into performance topics in "performance topics" your area of responsibility. Widespread application of this principle, along with cascading objectives and measures from level to level, ensures vertical alignment and gets everyone pulling in the same direction.

29.

FOCUS ON WHERE YOUR ORGANIZATION IS GOING & ... TRANSLATE FACTORS INTO PERFORMANCE TOPICS

# Stakeholders

Your second major source for choosing the right performance topics is your stakeholders. "Stakeholders" are simply those who have an significant stake in your performance and an ability to create consequences for you, good or bad. In using stakeholders as a source of performance topics, you examine your metrics from a totally different perspective— one that gives you the opportunity to validate, and perhaps extend, the metrics derived from your strategy.

Stockholders are one group of stakeholders at the corporate level, and there are many others. Depending on your position and the nature of your business, your stakeholders may include external customers, internal customers, shareholders, regulatory agencies, your community, a holding company, and others. Your primary stakeholders are the ones with legitimate interests in your performance and the ability to exert influence over you. It's important to consider them all; an ignored stakeholder is a potential time bomb for your organization, not to mention your career.

> "One thing is crucial to success in service, finding out who your customers are and what they expect."
>
> —O. Bjellandin

To get the right performance measures, you'll need to identify each stakeholder group, know its interests, and outline what is of value to that group. Think broadly about value so you include not only dollars, but also other kinds of value such as time, quality, risk, and so forth.

30.

*WHO ARE THE STAKEHOLDERS?*

*DON'T IGNORE ANY."*

"VALUE"

Many find "value creation" a useful perspective to adopt:

> *Our business is to create value for our stakeholders; our first job is to know who our stakeholders are and what they value in our performance.*

Here's the process:

- Identify all your stakeholders, internal and external to your organization.

- Conduct the appropriate research to find out what's important to each type of stakeholder. What does each consider "value" in your output or way of conducting business?

- Select which "valuable" things you will use as performance topics for your area of responsibility.

As with your strategy topics, you can apply the Three-Step Method to determine Critical Success Factors and performance indicators for each group of stakeholder values:

## Two Complementary Perspectives

| STRATEGY-MISSION-GOALS ANALYSIS | STAKEHOLDER ANALYSIS |
|---|---|
| Performance Topics | Identify Stakeholders |
| Critical Success Factors | What Do They Value? |
| Performance Indicators | Set Performance Topics |
| | Critical Success Factors |
| | Performance Indicators |

31.

# Snoozing Alligators

If you've examined your strategy and stakeholders, you are well along in finding the right performance topics. You may have most of your Primary Metrics. But there is one more type of performance topic you should consider, a controversial one.

Some say you should ignore topics that are not part of your strategy or relevant to your stakeholders. Focus on the critical few, they say. They're right. Focus is important; you cannot work on everything at once.

But a little careful thought will tell you it's not that simple. While you must put the focus on achieving strategic objectives, there are many other things that must be monitored. These topics, while not part of your strategy and perhaps not of concern to your stakeholders, are nevertheless crucial to your survival. These are topics that, if ignored, may someday rise up and bite your corporate backside. We sometimes call them "snoozing alligators," topics outside your immediate strategic focus, but ones you can't afford to ignore.

## "UNFORESEEN CHANGES"

Depending on your industry and circumstances, examples might include nearly anything: *Rate of Technology Adoption, Industrywide Production Capacity, Employee Satisfaction, Earnings in Constant Dollars*, etc.

Such alligators are important topics, to be sure, but maybe not specifically included in your strategy for the current period. Often you'll find these "alligators" are topics where no change is anticipated, yet where you certainly would want to know if even gradual changes were occurring. You might think of monitoring these alligators as a kind of internal vigilance that complements your external scanning activities.

> *"Major failures in business come not so much from unmet goals, as from lack of response to unforeseen changes."*
> –O. L. Duff

Only you know your situation well enough to identify these measurement topics. The point is that, while you begin with strategy and stakeholder topics, you may have to look outside these sources to measure all the topics important to your business.

Think carefully when you hear experts make compelling arguments for the "critical few" metrics. Remind yourself that they've never run a business like yours. In the end, you are far wiser to develop a design that spotlights the critical few but includes the critical many. You cannot afford to ignore snoozing alligators.

# Part 3

---

# Using Metrics to Improve Performance

- Reporting Performance

- Improving Performance

- Aligning Your Organization

- Managing Accountabilities

# Reporting Performance

There are three key words in reporting performance. They are *graphs, consistency* and *comparatives.*

In almost every case, *graphs* are the best way to present performance results. A picture is said to be worth a thousand words because we grasp meanings so much more quickly and easily in visual form. Graphs not only show you where you are, but where you've been and where you are likely to go. Use graphs and charts wherever you can.

> *"The great thing in this world is not so much where we stand, as in what direction we are moving."*
> –O. W. Holmes

The second essential in performance reporting is *consistency.* Your understanding of performance is more likely to be valid when:

- Your measurement definitions remain constant from period to period,

- Your charts show "up" as good, whenever possible; and

- Your methods of data collection and analysis remain stable from period to period.

Every improvement in your metrics must be weighed against the loss of period-to-period consistency that will result from adopting the improvement.

## " WHAT COMPARISONS?" " BENCHMARKS"

*Comparatives* are important because we judge things so poorly in the abstract; our minds are better geared to making comparison judgments. Your metrics need anchor points for these comparisons, benchmarks by which the results may be gauged. Examples might be your own past performance, your goals, customer expectations, etc. In particular, you should know how you compare to others in your industry and leaders in your particular area. Think carefully about what comparatives will lead you to valid conclusions and sensible action.

> *"You may be on the right road, but if you're not moving fast enough, you'll get run over!"*
> –B. Baker

The trend line offers a type of comparative that is generally very useful because it shows in what direction you are moving. When you show a trend line, you're implying that one comparative for your current performance is your past performance. Generally, that's a very good thing. However, let's also recognize that a single comparative is seldom enough. We usually need to know where we stand in other terms. In today's world, one may be doing consistently better than one did in the past, yet failing against one's competitors. And let's be clear about the fact that we all have competitors.

Because comparatives are so important, yet seldom given the attention they deserve, you'll find further discussion of them in a later section, Issues to Anticipate.

37.

# Improving Performance

It's clear how multidimensional performance scorecards are useful in two of your day to day leadership activities: making decisions and reporting performance.

But if you are an experienced manager or executive who's thought about it much, you also know performance metrics support two of your more complex leadership activities—implementing strategy and improving performance. More specifically, they are instrumental if you want to:

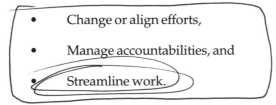

- Change or align efforts,

- Manage accountabilities, and

- Streamline work.

Let's save the streamlining topic for later and first consider the two leadership activities that most involve people—aligning effort and managing accountabilities.

# Aligning Effort

To understand how metrics help you change direction and align effort, consider a company we'll call GHI Transport. GHI offers passenger ferry service, containerized cargo, short-haul air freight, and trucking services. Several years ago, company leaders believed they could increase market share by improving service and becoming "customer focused." They used speeches, signs, slogans, newsletters and various educational efforts to get the word out. But change was painfully slow. While the new strategy seemed like a good idea, no one knew exactly what to do or whether any progress was being made.

To accelerate change, the executive group at GHI commissioned a special team to collect relevant performance measures directly from customers. The team charted these results and periodically gave detailed presentations throughout each line of business. This effort helped leaders at all levels give concrete meaning to the new strategy, dislodge old ways, and align effort behind it. The end result was dramatic change—in the desired direction—on a large scale.

The most basic means by which leaders improve performance involves making sure that everyone is working on the right things. Performance does not count unless it's related to the things that matter. You may get more

39.

accomplished, but your performance improves only if the added accomplishments are of value to your organization and its stakeholders.

Properly developed, metrics are like a glue that binds work throughout the organization to the larger goals.

Suppose *On-Time Delivery* is a key performance issue for your customer. But Sales, Purchasing, Assembly, Shipping and all others involved have differing objectives, budgets, and time constraints. By setting *On-Time Delivery to the Customer* as a key performance measure for everyone in the chain from order to delivery, you use a metric to align

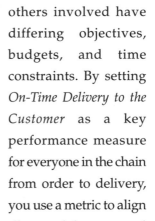

effort. Everyone is motivated to pull toward the same end result and to cooperate in achieving it. The overall goal is the same, but now everyone can be clear about what the "end result" really is. That makes all the difference. As a leader, you have taken a major step toward aligning effort behind the organization's strategy.

40.

The same principle applies in many other areas. By using the methods outlined earlier to develop your metrics, you can lay out a path by which your vision and direction for the organization, an intangible concept, will become concrete and achievable. In short, you have gauges and levers to create positive change.

The idea is simple enough. Execution is everything. You'll need to:

1) Be sure people know and understand the measures.

2) Collect the data fairly and report accurately.

3) Coach people when it's necessary.

4) Tie consequences, good and bad, to individual and team performance. Make the consequences visible.

Used this way, your performance metrics become a key tool for aligning your organization behind its strategic direction, dislodging the old ways, instituting the new, and getting everyone pulling in the right direction.

# Managing Accountabilities

Managing accountabilities is what people usually mean when they say "performance management." It includes the entire process:

✔ Defining jobs,

✔ Setting goals with individuals and groups,

✔ Tracking results,

✔ Reviewing performance,

✔ Providing rewards, and, yes. . .

✔ Kicking butts when necessary.

If managing accountabilities is central to improving performance, what's central to managing accountabilities? The answer: performance measures.

*"We promise according to our hopes, and perform according to our fears."*
–A. Lincoln

Measures speak a loud and clear message to people at all levels in an enterprise. They shout what really must get done. A picture may be worth a thousand words, and a performance chart is a picture of performance. It's certainly worth a thousand words about "objectives" and "goals."

There's something about performance charts. When most of us see a chart depicting our efforts, we immediately feel something—positive or negative. This feeling may be about the past or the future, but it's almost always motivational and emotional.

It's a useful feeling. The more we feel involved in the measuring and in control of the changes that are required, the more positive the motivation. Of course when measures are used to play "gotcha" with individuals or teams, they are rarely helpful.

If your employees know that you value metrics and track the entire organization's performance, an amazing thing happens. The culture changes. Whether mentally or on paper, employees begin to track how their own performance contributes to enterprise performance. And a "results-tracking culture" is one of the most powerful competitive advantages your enterprise can have.

RESULTS TRACKING CULTURE

For metrics to be motivational, people must be able to see what to do. There must be a *line of sight* between the actions employees can take and the changes that occur in the measure. For example, a product assembly team may find it easy to think in terms of hours per unit, but harder to see how their day-to-day efforts translate into changes in gross margin. In other words, this team has good line of sight to

43.

*Labor Hours Per Unit*, but a poor line of sight to *Gross Margin* for their product. The more clearly people see how they can affect the measure, the better.

When establishing rewards, you want to be particularly sure the line of sight principle holds. For example, you want sales commissions to result from higher volumes, not from territory rearrangements or the approval of price increases. The principle is self-evident. Rigorously applying it requires a watchful eye and, sometimes, difficult choices.

Before leaving, let's note that purely informational measures (that is, metrics with no line of sight) can sometimes be very useful, especially to those in senior management or planning positions. However, being held accountable for measures with no clear means to affect them is demotivating at any level.

"LINE OF SIGHT"

# Part 4

---

# Advanced Metrics

- Gaining Leverage

- Process Metrics

- Capability Metrics

# Gaining Leverage

Earlier, we referred to a third way to improve performance—"streamlining work" or, in modern terms, process management. This is radically different from managing accountabilities, and so are the metrics that support it. Process management goes beyond aligning effort and managing people. It addresses a completely different side of managing performance—managing the work processes and the strategic or "core" capabilities of your organization. It can help leaders stop spinning wheels, avoid waste, get more output for given input, and prepare for the future.

Our Leverage Model illustrates this principle:

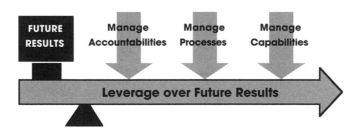

**The Leverage Model**

FUTURE RESULTS — Manage Accountabilities — Manage Processes — Manage Capabilities

**Leverage over Future Results**

As it applies to performance management, leverage is a profoundly significant principle. By measuring and managing a work *process*, you alter all the future results produced by that process. Likewise, by measuring and managing an *organizational capability*, you can influence all the future processes and results that rely on that capability.

Leverage over future results increases as you go further and further behind the scenes to manage the factors by which results are produced. Leverage first applies when you manage the accountability for results, then more broadly when you manage the work processes, and reaches its maximum when you manage the capabilities of your enterprise.

This powerful, increasing leverage is the reason *process management* has become such a hot topic in recent years.

MANAGE
ACCOUNTABILITY
FOR
RESULTS
→

MANAGE
WORK
PROCESSES
→

MANAGE
CAPABILITIES
→

" LEVERAGE "
OVER FUTURE
RESULTS .

47.

# Process Metrics

Process management is based on the idea of "work smarter, not harder." It calls for an overall, end-to-end view of work as a process—a sequence of stages and activities. Performance metrics illuminate this view.

Consider the approval of mortgage applications. A company we'll call SL Mortgage employed a convoluted process that involved many sub-departments, each with its own rules, and a work cycle that routed and re-routed work from desk to desk. Approvals took an average of *three months*. At the same time, industry experts said the actual work time in approving a mortgage totaled less than two hours—the rest was in hand-offs, wait time, and inefficiencies.

> *"The measure of success is not whether you have a problem to deal with, but whether it's the same problem you had last year."*
> –J. F. Dulles

SL Mortgage knew customers were dissatisfied with the delays, but the real wake-up call came when a competitor advertised three-day approvals!

The point is that the long approval cycle at SL Mortgage did not depend on how hard people were working or what they were accountable for. The long cycle resulted directly from *how the work was done*.

Consider another type of work, product development. In some industries, such as computer software, being first to market with a strong product means everything. You get the

48.

lion's share of the market and virtually all the earnings. Imagine the gains possible from a sleek, effective process for developing new products *and* getting them to market. Imagine the penalties you would pay for using a cumbersome, inefficient process.

Many think the process approach applies only to manufacturing work. Don't be fooled. It applies to all work.

Here, simplified, is the methodology for Process Management:

1) Define an end-to-end process that results in something of value to a stakeholder.

2) Determine what characteristics represent value on the receiving end. Usually these are a mix of quantity, quality, time, and cost factors.

3) Trace the flow of work from input to output, measuring the valued characteristics end-to-end and at each stage. Actually write down the process to get a visual picture of steps and handoffs, decision points, etc.

4) Redesign the process to improve performance on the end-to-end metrics—reduce handoffs, eliminate waits, errors, rework, bottlenecks, and lost

productivity. Eliminate non-value-added activities and steps.

As noted, your process metrics will normally represent four aspects of process performance—quantity, quality, time, and cost. Note that we're now talking about the performance of a process, not the performance of individuals or groups.

Although process metrics should conform to the line-of-sight principle wherever possible, you may find it necessary to balance this requirement against the fact that the ideal process metrics are broad measures tied directly to what the end user values. Such measures give you the most power to improve a process. In product development, for example, it's more powerful if you can measure from the point at which managers begin to evaluate a product concept than later, when designers actually begin drafting. The strategic issue at stake is partly how long it takes your designers to craft a product but also, and more importantly, how long it takes your organization to go from concept to revenue.

The bottom line on Process Metrics? They are advanced measures that bring new understandings of your performance and a powerful kind of leverage over results.

# Capability Metrics

For most organizations, enterprise capabilities represent a new frontier in performance metrics. Leaders are becoming concerned about measuring and managing organization-wide capabilities, or core competencies, based in part on the conceptual breakthroughs in strategy formulated by Drs. Gary Hamel and C. K. Prahalad.

Your metrics for managing capabilities will be your most advanced and high-level ones. The challenge in developing them is significant, but so is your additional leverage over future results.

At the enterprise level, Capability Metrics help you gauge and improve in broad areas like agility, scientific excellence, rapid product development, or any topic that represents either a competitive advantage or an ability to create better results in the future. For example, their capabilities in innovation and rapid development led to performance accolades from the Department of Defense for a contractor that was able to quickly develop and deliver a special "bunker buster" weapon during Desert Storm. Likewise, a new capability for managing risk, say by use of an improved statistical model, might be an advantage in the insurance industry.

Capability management is also practiced less formally. For example, you may realize that future earnings, or survival, depend on increasing your capability in a certain area like photolithography, performance metrics, or semiconductor design. So you set about hiring or training a nucleus of individuals in that area. For a more complex example, your business unit may realize that its agility, or ability to deploy change quickly, will be an important competitive advantage in the future. So you set about measuring and managing how change occurs in the business.

This is what's new: The idea that you can actually measure and manage organizational capabilities (whether you mean agility or photolithography) and can consciously adjust your core competencies to improve future performance. When successful, the leverage you gain over results is enormous.

Though Capability Metrics represent a frontier in measurement, the general method for using them is clear:

1) **Determine the competencies and capabilities** that will optimize your future. These should flow from your strategy or the thinking behind your strategy.

2) **Develop measurement methods** for these capabilities and begin tracking them. This will likely require new thinking and experimentation.

53.

3) **Benchmark the competencies and capabilities;**
Identify examples of excellence. Establish the
comparatives and best practices by which you will
judge your performance. Use gap analysis to
document your competitive position and
development needs.

4) **Set objectives and close the gaps.**

# Part 5

---

# Issues to Anticipate

# What Lies Ahead?

Perfecting your performance metrics will present you with numerous questions and issues. A few of them are:

1)   How many measures should you have?

2)   How often should you measure?

3)   What about shared accountabilities?

4)   Could your measures be contaminated?

5)   Are your measures reliable?

6)   Which performance comparatives are best?

7)   Should you combine measures into an index?

8)   Is "denominator management" a risk?

9)   How can good measures be made better?

Whether this is the first time you've thought about performance measures or you are well experienced in tracking enterprise performance, you will be challenged by these issues. Let's take them up one at a time.

# How Many Measures?

Everyone wants the right number of metrics. Some authorities even recommend fixed limits—10 to 15 measures, never more than eight, etc.

The reason, of course, is that leaders do not want to overwhelm their organizations with too many measures. Action-oriented leaders want to measure and manage the "critical few" things that will really make a difference.

But there are three deadly arguments against arbitrarily limiting the number of metrics:

1) First, there are the snoozing alligators. Things you must monitor, even if they may not change.

2) Second, there's complexity. Modern organizations are large and complex. Leaders need comprehensive pictures of performance to guide understandings and decisions. Managing with a keyhole view can lead to disaster.

Ever look into the cockpit as you are boarding a flight? You probably saw that the pilot and copilot face a hundred or more dials and gauges. Would you want to limit them to 8-15?

Actually, only a few gauges are important to a pilot at any one time. The airspeed indicator is not important while the plane is at the gate, for example.

57.

And only a few gauges are critical during takeoff or landing. And only a few at cruising altitude. But they're not the same few! The critical few change with conditions, so the pilot needs, in total, a full complement of gauges.

And it's the same with performance metrics in a large organization. Not all of your metrics will demand focused attention all the time, but if a few key ones are missing, your organization could be heading for a nosedive without realizing it.

3)  Third, there's the rob-Peter-to-pay-Paul problem. Stated simply: Anything not measured is subject to being sacrificed for the things that are measured. From a management perspective, this is a powerful argument for comprehensive metrics. One side of the coin says, "What gets measured, gets done." The other side says "What doesn't get measured, might not get done." And some of what might not get done can be darned important.

No one would do this. . . . But think what could happen to long-term research and product development if everyone in your organization was a year from retirement and you measured and compensated everyone solely on quarter-by-quarter earnings?

Your challenge in establishing performance metrics is to ensure that everything important at your level of the organization is represented and monitored, *and* that the critical few occupy center stage.

Is there any help? Yes. You might consider the designs of others who've solved, or partly solved, this problem. Some of the more common solutions involve foreground and background metrics; tiers of metrics available by drill-down links; and designs that distinguish between strategic metrics and monitored metrics. Special software packages have also been developed for managing a large number of metrics while keeping the focus on a critical few.

# How Often to Measure?

How often should you take readings on your performance indicators? In practice, this question is more complex than you might think.

The right answer is unique to each measure. But the guiding principles for framing your answer are clear:

1)  Other things being equal, you measure according to the rate of change you expect in the results. No point in measuring productivity every half hour, is there? But every month? Maybe. It depends on the nature of your work.

2)  The more you have at stake, the more often you measure. Even when you expect little change, additional tracking may be worth the price as a precaution. Aircraft pilots frequently check their altimeters!

3)  The longer it takes to respond, the more often you need to measure and the more finely tuned your metrics must be. You need the additional lead time. Before radar, the captains of large vessels checked for icebergs very frequently. When it takes a long time to alter course, your corrective action must begin at the earliest possible moment.

4) The more short-term variability in your results,
the more you want to average over time to separate
what's really happening from the short-term
changes. One or two satisfied, or dissatisfied,
customers among thousands do not make a trend.

5) Then there are administrative and political factors.
You may be required to report results more
frequently than you would otherwise feel the need
to measure.

There is no formula for how often to measure because each
situation is different. But the principles are clear and those
closest to the action must apply them to establish the right
measurement frequency.

# Shared Accountability?

In using metrics to manage performance, the matter of shared versus individual accountabilities has sometimes perplexed organizations.

Some leaders take a conservative position, holding to the idea that every measure and every accountability must be associated with a single individual or it's of no use. Others believe some objectives require, by their nature, the sharing of accountability.

Certainly, it's easy to agree with the principle of individual accountability. But what about those performance objectives that cannot be accomplished by one person or, in some cases, even by several? Consider workplace safety, total shareholder return, customer satisfaction, or a positive work climate. Someone may be responsible for the metrics that report on such matters, but often that person cannot be held solely accountable for achieving the results. Nor can we simply leave out such metrics. Important things do not go away just because we find them difficult to measure or manage.

Some leaders have found part of the solution by sharpening the distinctions they make among the managerial terms *authority, responsibility*, and *accountability*. They suggest authority is the right to act without prior approval from higher management and without challenge from peers.

Responsibility, then, is an obligation to perform. Accountability is the liability one assumes for ensuring that an obligation to perform—a responsibility—is fulfilled. In this system, then:

- Responsibility can be delegated.

- Authority is assigned.

- Accountability cannot be delegated, but can be shared.

What is the bottom line? Enterprise strategies, goals, and objectives must be measured to be managed. As many as possible become individual accountabilities, others are shared. Those accountable may delegate responsibility to one or many to perform, but they remain liable. Results are reported by those who are in the best position to collect and summarize relevant data.

# Contamination

In the world of performance metrics, validity means that a measure tracks what it's supposed to and is not contaminated by other factors that render your conclusions uncertain or invalid.

Consider a widely used, but highly contaminated, productivity indicator—*Sales Per Employee*, or likewise, *Earnings Per Employee*. The contamination in such indicators is clear when you consider how these ratios behave over time. Because the value of money varies over time, these productivity indicators become rubber rulers when you plot trends. Times of inflation make it appear that productivity is improving even if it's not; the opposite occurs in times of deflation. Ideally, you want to define performance indicators so they are not subject to such outside influences. In this example, a less contaminated indicator might be *Earnings Per $1000 of Payroll*—a ratio in which inflation tends to work on both the numerator and denominator.

*"There are three kinds of lies: Lies, damned lies, and statistics."*
–B. Disraeli

Another kind of validity problem comes from looking in the wrong place for answers. Consider an online transaction processing system that operates round the clock to serve customers. If you track *Computer Uptime* as a system performance indicator, you will overestimate how the system actually performs for customers. That's because

64.

failures and delays occur primarily under high loads at certain times of the day. Failures at such times affect many more customers than failures at other times, but the indicator counts all seconds of uptime as equal, whether they are at 5:00 PM or midnight. In this case, an indicator that tracks the proportion of possible customer transactions for which the system is ready to perform would express performance *in terms relevant to the business.*

You'll want your performance indicators carefully scrutinized by critically-minded persons or experienced experts to root out all possible contaminations. After all, perhaps the only thing worse than no measurement is false measurement. You do not want to expend a great deal of effort "correcting" a trend that doesn't need correcting. Nor do you want to think that everything is going fine when, in reality, a problem is emerging.

# Reliability

Reliability, an extremely desirable characteristic in all performance indicators, has a simple meaning in practice. A reliable indicator is one that produces the same result every time, given the same circumstances.

But the circumstances never are *exactly* the same from one time to the next. In addition, every way of measuring has built in variation coming from the methods employed. Readings always vary somewhat from the "true" answer. Only in an ideal world is any performance indicator 100% reliable. The good news? Reliability is controllable.

Consider one common reason for unreliability—sample size. If a measurement sample is too small, you are not grouping enough readings to "wash out" the variation that's naturally present. Suppose you sample only six items from a group of 2000 for defects. Or you sample six of 2000 employees in a survey on working conditions. In either case, you're likely to get a different answer when you draw another sample of six, even if nothing has changed. Your sampling method is creating a situation of low measurement reliability. On the other hand, imagine that you randomly sample 1000 of the 2000. You'll get the same result when you sample the other 1000 because you are averaging over such large numbers. The same might hold with samples of 500 or 200. The best way to know that you're sampling just enough to get reliable results generally is to consult an expert in sampling statistics. Perhaps there's one in your organization; or it may be worthwhile to consult a measurement expert to help you set up reliable measures.

Sample size is only one of the pitfalls in creating reliable measures. Others are specific to the things you are measuring. You will want to examine your metrics for ways in which they may prove unreliable and, in some cases, even run a test on their reliability. If you take action based on unreliable measures, you will not correct a situation, but are likely to make it worse. Deming calls this type of premature management action "tampering."

Consider the large bank we'll call CSH. On one of their performance measures, errors were so few that the goal called for improving accuracy from 95% to 96% over the course of a year. Progress was carefully monitored by senior management and people were held

> *"It ain't so much the things we don't know that get us in trouble. It's the things we know that ain't so."*
> –A. Ward

accountable. When performance dropped one month (from 95.5% to 95.3%), people were "called on the carpet." Unfortunately, CSH staff did not compute and report the appropriate statistics relating to reliability—so CSH executives were led to believe every difference, however small, represented a real change in performance. The bottom line is that, unless you take reliability into account, there's no way to tell whether taking quick action means you are on top of things or it means you are jumping at shadows.

# Comparatives

You might think that defining your performance indicators and getting the data would be all there is to measurement. But it's not so. You still have to figure out how you're doing—what to conclude from the measures you track. Data, by itself, doesn't tell you much.

You need benchmarks and anchors, comparatives, as standards by which to judge what your indicators show. Countless studies on judgment and decision making confirm what we know from everyday experience—people are very poor at evaluating things in the abstract. We are better at comparing things. Is $179,900 high or low for a certain house? The realtor searches for "comparables." Is 8,267 units of production good or bad? The supervisor checks results from other days.

Because your comparatives have so much impact on the conclusions you reach, they're actually as important as your performance indicators. This is particularly true when you realize performance will look strong when you put results up against one comparative, middling compared to another, and poor compared to a third.

What is a good comparative? Finding the right one begins with understanding your options. Basically, there are three types of comparatives: *internal*, *external*, and *theoretical*.

1) **Internal comparatives,** those most commonly used,
   contrast your present performance to other standards
   inside your organization. They might include your
   past performance, goals you've set, targets you are
   trying to reach, etc.

2) **External comparatives,** though not always fully
   comparable to your measures, are of great value
   in a business sense. They might include the
   performance of competitors or of vendors who
   perform similar services.

3) **Theoretical standards** are more important than you
   would think, particularly in measuring work
   processes. As an example, consider a work process
   with several stages and activities. We can study each
   stage and add up the total actual work time in the
   process. This becomes the minimum possible time
   for the process—a theoretical standard. The actual
   time for a work cycle is always longer because of
   handoffs, wait time, and other factors. If we compare
   the actual cycle time to the theoretical minimum, we
   can check the result against published reports for
   world-class performance. In manufacturing work,
   for example, world-class performers show cycle
   times that are about twice the theoretical
   minimums. In administrative work, world class
   performance is said to be about five times the
   theoretical minimums!

Let's summarize three main points about comparatives:

1) Comparatives have an immense impact on the accuracy and fairness of your judgments about performance.

2) You need to consider the full range of comparatives and whether better comparatives might lead to better understandings of performance.

3) Combining comparatives allows you to paint richer pictures of performance. You might, for example, display a performance trend line and also show goals for each time period and external benchmarks—allowing current performance to be immediately, visually compared to past performance, a goal, and an external benchmark.

Measuring Performance

# The Performance Index

In measuring performance, you are sure to encounter the controversial subject of the performance index. Some people are for them, and some are against. An index is a composite number you create by mathematically combining several individual measures. Each measure is multiplied by a factor to give it a weighting in the composite. The Dow Jones Industrials Average (DJIA) is a well-known index representing a weighted group of individual stocks.

The arguments in favor of using a performance index come down to ease and efficiency. People sometimes want to see one number that sums up the performance of many things. That way they have fewer things to watch. When the index changes, they know it may be time to take action.

The arguments against using a performance index come down to the fact that it obscures important information. One measure in the index may goes up, and another down, but the index may stay the same.

For example, suppose you follow the DJIA in watching the stock market. It's possible for ten stocks in the DJIA to go up sharply, and ten down sharply at the same time, with no change in the index. As a general index, the DJIA is a good one; like other indices, it cannot tell you about changes that occur within the index.

If you were to combine all your performance indicators in a given category, say all your process measures, your index may not move at all if you have cycle time improvements that are just enough to balance an increase in defects. Nothing appears to be happening, and a false sense of security may set in. In short, the index is masking information contained in the specific metrics, so the metrics aren't able to do their job of alerting and informing.

For a given situation, you'll have to judge whether or not the problem of obscuring important information outweighs the value of using an index. Careful design can always help minimize your risk but, other things being equal, those who use metrics day to day for implementing strategy and improving performance will want to see individual indicators rather than composites.

# Denominator Management

Ratio measures are susceptible to a unique problem called "denominator management."

It works like this. You set an objective, such as reducing defects. Because you want to compare performance across situations with differing volumes, you choose to track not defects, but a ratio like *Defects per Million Opportunities*. People everywhere begin catching and eliminating defects. The ratio gets better.

After the "low hanging fruit" is picked, defects become harder to eliminate and a curious thing happens. Because everyone wants the ratio to drop further, people begin directing their activities toward the denominator of the measure, discovering additional millions of opportunities for defects that belong in the denominator. This is managing the denominator, rather than the numerator, or "denominator management." It's wasted effort, directed toward improving the metric itself rather than toward your original objective of reducing defects.

Take another example. Productivity metrics are normally set with the end in mind of increasing output in an efficient manner. Because productivity is a ratio of output divided by input, managers often work both on increasing the output and on reducing the input. All well and good. Except that some people just work the denominator—putting all their attention on strangling input. Likewise, others are tempted to forego small, near-term investments that will create much greater output in the future.

To a greater or lesser degree, denominator management occurs with all performance indicators that employ ratios. When denominator management is observed, it often indicates you've hit a ceiling and there's not much more room for the kind of improvement you are seeking. Chances are, it's time to turn your attention to a new aspect of performance.

What are the lessons learned?

✔ Metrics can easily generate unintended behaviors.

✔ People must sign on for the true objective, not just for the metric.

✔ The behavioral impacts of performance metrics must be continually rechecked.

✔ The point of diminishing returns should be recognized.

✔ Consider avoiding ratio measures when you have a choice.

# Making Good Metrics Better

As organizations begin establishing stronger performance metrics, many assume they'll be finished once the design is complete. You need to know that this isn't so.

If your experience follows that of others, you'll find that your measurement system needs ongoing improvements and modifications. The reasons include changes in strategy and circumstances, lack of perfect foresight, and improving concepts and approaches in the metrics discipline.

What are the lessons and implications?

1) **Think continuous improvement.** Design the best system you can at the outset, but recognize you'll want to improve it later.

2) **Plan annual reviews.** At least once a year, identify metrics issues and decide about improvements.

3) **Collect perspectives.** As experience, models, and examples accumulate, the metrics field continually advances. Stay abreast of what others are doing.

4) **Develop your roadmap.** Think ahead toward the next stages of performance management for your organization. What's next after you achieve strong vertical alignment? Will your plan call for resolving horizontal misalignments, broader process management, more attention to managing capabilities?

# Part 6

# Performance Management

# A Summary Model

Throughout this book, we've explored the relationship between metrics and the leader's job in managing performance. Let's collect and summarize our main points as concisely as possible:

1) Organizational performance today is managed more objectively than ever before. It relies on performance metrics.

2) Performance metrics are primarily derived from the strategy, mission, and goals of the organization and factors important to key stakeholders. Advanced metrics are derived from the factors necessary to improve work processes and organizational capabilities.

3) Metrics are central to at least four tasks leaders must perform: Report Performance, Make Decisions, Implement Strategy, and Improve Performance.

4) As leaders perform the four tasks that most rely on metrics, they can create positive organizational impacts at five or more points. They can achieve:

   • Rationalized resources

   • Clear accountabilities

   • Aligned effort

   • Efficient processes

   • Future capabilities.

Throughout this book, you've seen these concepts illustrated with simple diagrams. If you are one who likes to see the big picture, here's my last word as the author—or my last 1,000 words in the form of a picture. This diagram assembles the figures we've used into a more comprehensive view of strategy-based performance management. It illustrates the links that tie your enterprise strategies and goals to your metrics, to the leader's job in creating change and managing performance, and to the organizational impacts that result:

## Strategy-Based Performance Management

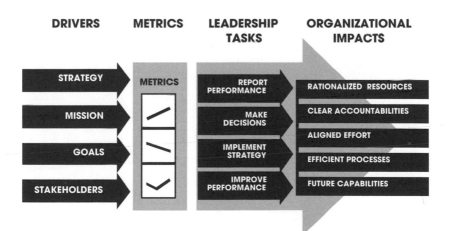

As you pursue the important work of translating strategy into action in your organization, please accept my best wishes in all that you do.

# Part 7

---

# Resources & Glossary

# References

You'll find an increasing number of books and a rapidly growing collection of articles on organizational metrics and strategy-based performance management. Many of the best have appeared in the Harvard Business Review, particularly since 1990. Here are the works we've referenced in this book along with a select group of the early, classic works in this field:

Cooper. R. and Kaplan, R.S. "Profit Priorities from Activity Based Costing," *Harvard Business Review,* May-June, 1991, 130-137.

Eccles R.G., Pyburn P.J. "Creating a Comprehensive System to Measure Performance," *Management Accounting,* pg.41-44, October, 1992.

Eccles, R.G. "The Performance Measurement Manifesto," *Harvard Business Review,* January-February, 1991, 131-137. Reprint 91103.

Hamel, G. and Prahalad, C.K. *Competing for the Future.* Cambridge, MA: Harvard Business School Press, 1987. ISBN: 0-87584-416-2.

Johnson, H. T. and Kaplan, R. S. *Relevance Lost–The Rise and Fall of Management Accounting.* Boston, MA Harvard Business School Press, 1987.

Kaplan, R.S. "Yesterday's Accounting Undermines Production," *Harvard Business Review,* 62, 1984, 95-101.

Kaplan, R.S. and Norton, D.P. "The Balanced Scorecard - Measures that Drive Performance," *Harvard Business Review,* January-February, 1992, 71-79.

Keegan, D.P., Jones, C.R., and Eiler, R.G. "To Implement Your Strategies, Change Your Measurements," *Price Waterhouse Reprint,* Number 1, 1991.

Keegan, D.P., Eiler, R.G. and Jones, C.R. "Are Your Performance Measures Obsolete?" *Management Accounting,* June, 1989, 45-50.

Lynch, R.L. & Cross, K.F. *Measure up!: Yardsticks for Continuous Improvement.* Cambridge, MA: Blackwell Publishers, 1991. ISBN 1-55786-461-6.

*METC Performance Improvement Measurement Methodology.* U.S. Department of Energy, Morgantown Energy Technical Center, 1994. (www.metc.doe.gov/tqm)

Meyers, R. "Getting a Grip on Intangibles," *CFO Magazine,* September, 1996.

Mills, R. and Print, C. "Strategic Value Analysis: Shareholder Value and Economic Value Added - What's the Difference?" *Management Accounting,* 73, 2, 1995, 35-36.

Sink, D.S. and Tuttle, T.C. *Planning and Measurement in Your Organization of the Future.* Norcross, GA: Industrial Engineering and Management Press, 1989.

Thor, C.G. *The Measures of Success: Creating a High Performance Organization.* Essex Junction, VT: Oliver Wright Publications, Inc., 1994.

*Metrics: A Management Guide.* Texas Instruments Inc., Dallas, TX, 1997. Moore Business Forms, Dallas, TX, #TI-29820.

# Glossary

Because performance metrics and multidimensional performance scorecards are relatively new, you'll find distinctions sometimes blurred and terms used in various ways. Here's an informal glossary covering some of the most important terms:

**Activity Based Costing (ABC)** – ABC is a method of analyzing and understanding costs that attempts to assign costs according to the actual resources consumed rather than arbitrary spreading according to formulas.

**Advanced Metrics** – As used here, Advanced Metrics are those used in measuring and managing work processes and organizational capabilities. Examples are *Cycle Time, Defects Per Unit*, and *Agility*.

**Align** – Alignment of work means activities in different areas all support the same overall goals. Vertical alignment means performance metrics in each area are derived from a common base (for example, an organization's strategic objective in rapid product development) and serve to align work efforts.

**Balanced Scorecard** – A model that groups multidimensional performance metrics into the categories of Financial, Customer, Internal Processes, and Future (or Learning and Growth) metrics.

**Capability** – The resources or capacity to perform in a certain way. *Photolithography, Risk Management, Agility, Production Planning*, etc. are examples.

**Comparative** – Comparatives are the benchmarks or anchors used in judging measured performance. Examples are past performance, world-class benchmarks, competitor performance, etc.

**Consistency** – Consistency means that all the data for a given metric are defined, collected and reported similarly so that results are easier to interpret and comparisons over time are more likely to be valid.

**Contamination** – Contamination is the operation of factors that are not accounted for and that render conclusions invalid. For example, inflation sometimes contaminates metrics denominated in dollars.

**Critical Success Factors (CSF)** – CSFs are the sub-topics that spell out where the organization must succeed on a major performance topic. Examples might include wait time as part of customer service, or leasing activities as a part of earnings.

**Cross-functional** – Cross-functional refers to a metric that spans several departments. *Order-to-Delivery Cycle Time* would be an example.

**Cycle Time** – Cycle time is the interval from the beginning to the end of a defined process. *Circuit Card Assembly Cycle Time, Order Entry to Shipping Cycle Time, Product Introduction Cycle Time, Report Preparation Cycle Time* are examples.

**Denominator** – The denominator is the portion of a fraction or ratio below the dividing line. In a productivity measure like *Items Processed per Hour*, the number of hours would be the denominator.

**Denominator Management** – Denominator Management refers to actions that improve a performance measure, but not through progress on the desired goal. Reducing *Defects Per Million Opportunities* by finding more opportunities where defects could have occurred would be an example.

**Economic Value Added (EVA)** – EVA is a way of measuring financial performance that calculates the value added by an enterprise above and beyond the value of the capital used by the enterprise.

**Enterprise Resource Planning (ERP)** – ERP refers to large-scale efforts that centrally warehouse data for widespread use. For example, order entry data would be readily accessible by the shipping department so a proper inventory of packaging materials could be maintained.

**Line of sight** – Line of sight means those who are accountable for a given type of performance can see how their day-to-day actions directly affect the performance indicator.

**Index** – An index mathematically combines the results of several measures into a single composite number.

**Measurement error** – Measurement error is the amount by which a measured result differs from its "true" value because of random variation or the design of the measurement process.

**Metric, Measure, Performance Indicator** – These three terms are often used interchangeably in the developing field of performance management. Those who distinguish among them say that "metric" is the unit of measure, "measure" means a specific observation characterizing performance, and "performance indicator" is a specifically defined variable.

**Multidimensional** – Multidimensional means a collection of measures that take several perspectives. The Balanced Scorecard, for example, is one model for multidimensional measures of organizational performance.

**Numerator** – The numerator is the portion of a ratio above the dividing line. In a productivity measure like *Items Processed per Hour*, the total items processed would be the numerator.

**Performance Topic** – A general subject area on which the organization has determined that its accomplishments are important. Examples might include shareholder return, customer service, productivity, etc.

**Primary Metrics** – As used here, Primary Metrics are those derived from strategy, mission, goals, and stakeholder values. Though primary metrics can include process measures if they reflect the organization's strategy, they generally track the results the organization intends to produce. Primary Metrics such as *Earnings, Customer Satisfaction, On-time Delivery,* etc. are used in managing individual and group accountabilities.

**Process** – A group of sequenced work activities with a defined beginning and end.

**Process Management** – Process Management is a management approach that includes defining end-to-end work processes, mapping activities within the process, measuring process and sub-process performance, and redesigning to improve process performance.

**Reliability** – Perfect reliability means a performance indicator produces the same result under identical measuring conditions. Reliability is reduced when inconsistent methods are employed, sample sizes are too small, or other methodological flaws are introduced.

**Strategy** – Strategy means a planned approach to gaining advantage, a plan for how the organization will prevail over competitors and obstacles. In practice, considerable variation exists in what organizations consider "strategy."

**Stakeholder** – A stakeholder is a person or group with a vested interest in your performance. For a line of business, stakeholders would include customers, employees, suppliers, regulators, etc. Many of the same stakeholder groups apply at the department level, as well as additional stakeholders within the enterprise.

**Unidimensional** – Unidimensional refers to a set of metrics that all reflect a single perspective on performance. For example, a set of performance metrics that contains only financial measures.

**Validity** –At bottom, validity means your measures reflect what you say they reflect and are not influenced by the operation of contaminating factors.

Measuring Performance

94.

Measuring Performance

# A final note. . .

We hope you find this primer as useful in your organization as we have in our practice at Measurement International. For other books in this series, please visit: www.MeasurementInternational.com.

For information on the support services offered by Measurement International for implementing strategy-based performance management—including a range of advisory, project, and design review services—please contact our office at 214-350-1082.

# Additional copies. . .

For fast service on multiple copies or bulk orders of *Measuring Performance*, phone the publisher direct at 214-350-1082. Please be prepared to provide the following information:

Number of copies required: _____

Name: _____

Title: _____

Company: _____

Address: _____

City, State, ZIP: _____

Phone:_____ E-mail:_____